YEAR ONE:
BATMAN

Dan DiDio   Senior VP-Executive Editor
Nachie Castro   Editor-original series
Robert Greenberger   Senior Editor-collected edition
Robbin Brosterman   Senior Art Director
Paul Levitz   President & Publisher
Georg Brewer   VP-Design & DC Direct Creative
Richard Bruning   Senior VP-Creative Director
Patrick Caldon   Executive VP-Finance & Operations
Chris Caramalis   VP-Finance
John Cunningham   VP-Marketing
Terri Cunningham   VP-Managing Editor
Stephanie Fierman   Senior VP-Sales & Marketing
Alison Gill   VP-Manufacturing
Rich Johnson   VP-Book Trade Sales
Hank Kanalz   VP-General Manager, WildStorm
Lillian Laserson   Senior VP & General Counsel
Jim Lee   Editorial Director-WildStorm
Paula Lowitt   Senior VP-Business & Legal Affairs
David McKillips   VP-Advertising & Custom Publishing
John Nee   VP-Business Development
Gregory Noveck   Senior VP-Creative Affairs
Cheryl Rubin   Senior VP-Brand Management
Jeff Trojan   VP-Business Development, DC Direct
Bob Wayne   VP-Sales

YEAR ONE: BATMAN/RA'S AL GHUL
Published by DC Comics. Cover and compilation
copyright © 2006 DC Comics. All Rights Reserved.
Originally published in single magazine form in YEAR
ONE: BATMAN/RA'S AL GHUL #1-2. Copyright
© 2005 DC Comics. All Rights Reserved. All
characters, their distinctive likenesses and related elements
featured in this publication are trademarks of DC Comics.
The stories, characters and incidents featured in this
publication are entirely fictional. DC Comics does not
read or accept unsolicited submissions of ideas, stories or
artwork. DC Comics, 1700 Broadway, New York, NY
10019. A Warner Bros. Entertainment Company. Printed
in Canada. First Printing.
ISBN: 1-4012-0904-1
ISBN-13: 978-1-4012-0904-9

Cover illustration by Paul Gulacy
Cover color by Laurie Kronenberg
Logo design by Terry Marks
Publication design by John J. Hill

WRITER **DEVIN GRAYSON**

PENCILLER **PAUL GULACY**

INKER **JIMMY PALMIOTTI**

COLORIST **LAURIE KRONENBERG**

RA'S AL GHUL

LETTERER **PHIL BALSMAN**

ORIGINAL COVERS **PAUL GULACY**
& **JIMMY PALMIOTTI**

BATMAN CREATED BY **BOB KANE**

BATMAN

A family outing to the cinema ended in tragedy for eight-year-old Bruce Wayne when Dr. Thomas Wayne and his wife Martha were killed by a mugger on a street known today as Crime Alley. Bruce witnessed the act and his life changed irrevocably. Bruce swore a solemn oath to avenge his parents' deaths and he continued to live in Wayne Manor, tended to by the family valet Alfred Pennyworth. At age 14, Bruce embarked on a journey that took him to every continent, crisscrossing the globe several times over as he sought to learn every skill he would need to keep his vow. He audited courses at Cambridge and the Sorbonne. He studied criminology, forensics, and the psychology of the criminal mind. Under assumed names, Bruce apprenticed with manhunters and martial artists, learning the subtleties of detection and deduction while mastering every known fighting style. Upon his return to Gotham City, Bruce began to operate outside the law. In short order, he learned he needed a disguise to strike fear in criminal hearts. When a bat crashed through the Manor's window, he was inspired to create that disguise and so the Batman was born. In the twelve years since that night, the Batman has become not only Gotham City's protector but an inspiration for others ranging from the police force to Dick Grayson, who became the first Robin and is now Nightwing; Barbara Gordon, who became the first Batgirl and is now Oracle; and Tim Drake, the current Robin. Along the way he has encountered some of the most dangerous, grotesque and deadly foes imaginable. He and Gotham have survived much, starting with political corruption but even a plague, an earthquake and a year-long exile from the United States. And both have endured. Bruce Wayne is now a shell, a disguise to service the Batman's unending quest to give the people of Gotham City a protector against the criminal element's violence and madness.

The first recorded appearance of the man who is now known as Ra's al Ghul dates back over 600 years. Born to a tribe of Arabian desert nomads, he expressed an interest in science and left the tribe to live and pursue his research in a city. There, he met and married Sora. As a practicing physician, he discovered the alchemical combination of ingredients, harvested from the ground above electro-magnetic ley lines that crisscross the planet, and built his first Lazarus Pit in order to save a dying prince. Driven insane by the body's rejuvenation, the sadistic prince strangled Sora. The prince's father charged the doctor, not the prince, with the murder and he was imprisoned with his wife's corpse. He escaped and took revenge — first killing the king and prince with his advanced scientific knowledge and then burning the city. He then took the name Ra's al Ghul, which translates to "Demon's Head." Using the Lazarus Pits to keep himself alive, Ra's spent the next several centuries traveling the world and increasing his knowledge. During this time he built many organizations, the best known being the League of Assassins. Over time, he watched, in horror, as the industrialized world began to poison the planet. Finally, he found his true calling and has set out to rid the world of most of humanity, so the ecosystem may heal itself and return Earth to a place of splendor. With the years, though, Ra's recognized that the Pits would not keep him alive forever and needed to begin building a succession plan, which brought the Batman to his attention. When Batman refused the role of heir and son-in-law, the two began a series of confrontations that grew deadlier with each meeting. Ra's never allowed himself to love again but has raised at least two daughters. The first, Nyssa, grew to hate him for his cold, unfeeling way and recently, she kidnapped her half sister, Talia, and brainwashed her, turning her into an instrument of revenge. Talia killed their father, which triggered the events in the following tale.

RA'S AL GHUL

YES, ALFRED?

DEET *DEET*

DEEEET

I DO HOPE I AM NOT INTERRUPTING ANY **EXCESSIVELY** VIOLENT ACTIVITIES, SIR...

YOU MISSED THE **EXCESSIVE** VIOLENCE BY EIGHT SECONDS...

IT'S NEGATIVE FOR KNOWN TOXICITIES...

STILL, STAND BACK, JUST IN CASE.

OH, BUT IT WOULD BE IN SUCH POOR TASTE TO LET YOU DIE ALONE *NOW,* MASTER BRUCE.

AND IN ANY CASE, WE SEEM TO BE IN LUCK.

IT'S MERELY A LETTER.

A POST-HUMOUS LETTER FROM RA'S AL GHUL...

...."LUCK" ISN'T EXACTLY WHAT I THINK WE'RE ABOUT TO BE IN.

19 JULY 2001,
CAIRO

MY DEAR
DETECTIVE--

THOUGH I CANNOT HELP BUT HOPE THAT
THE DELIVERY OF THIS LETTER PROVES
UNNECESSARY, I WRITE IT NOW WITH THE
GREAT COMPASSION AND RESPECT I
HAVE ALWAYS FELT TOWARDS YOU.

IT IS STILL MY INTENTION TO WIN YOU TO
MY CAUSE--NO MAN WITH YOUR
INTELLIGENCE COULD FAIL TO SEE THE
ABSOLUTE INTERDEPENDENCY OF ALL LIFE
ON THIS PLANET AND THE FINAL NECESSITY
OF PROTECTING THE LARGER ORGANISM
OF WHICH WE ARE SO SMALL A PART--

--BUT I WOULD BE FOOLISH NOT
TO PLAN FOR THE POSSIBILITY OF
MY DEFEAT AT YOUR HANDS PRIOR
TO OUR METHODOLOGY BEING
BROUGHT INTO ACCORD.

AND SO, A WARNING...

THE LAZARUS PITS, DETECTIVE, ARE NOT WHAT YOU SUPPOSE.

IT IS TRUE THAT, WHEN USED CAREFULLY, THEY CONFER A NEAR-PERFECT IMMORTALITY, AND ALSO, REGRETTABLY, A TEMPORARY TRACE OF INSANITY.

IT IS ALSO TRUE, AS YOU DEDUCED SO QUICKLY, THAT THE BLESSING OF HEALTH AND VITALITY THE SUBMERSIONS BESTOW ARE FINITE, COMPELLING THOSE WHO WOULD BE TRUE IMMORTALS TO SEEK OUT THE PITS WITH EVER-INCREASING FREQUENCY.

AND YET, STILL... THAT TERRIBLE INTERDEPENDENCY.

PERHAPS YOU SENSE AN INKLING OF IT IN YOUR SELF-IMPOSED DEVOTION TO YOUR THANKLESS MISTRESS.

YOU, WHO HAVE MANAGED TO BECOME GOTHAM CITY'S EYES AND HEART AND FISTS.

I SUPPOSE IT WAS THAT STRANGE SELF-METAMORPHOSIS--

--AS WELL AS MY DAUGHTER'S AFFECTION FOR YOU AND YOUR PROVEN INTELLIGENCE AND BRAVERY--

--THAT LEFT ME WITH SUCH HIGH HOPES FOR YOU.

THE COURTYARD'S BURNING, TOO!

OH GOD, STEVEN! WE'RE TRAPPED!

A MAN WHO ROUTINELY EXECUTES THE IMPOSSIBLE WOULD SURELY WANT A HAND IN THE NECESSARY AND INEVITABLE.

NEVER EVEN INGESTED REAL FOOD OR, DESPITE YOUR APPARENT FITNESS, KNOWN THE VITALITY OF A BODY FREE FROM THE TYRANNY OF TOXIC ONSLAUGHT.

NOW.

AS A SON OF THE TWENTIETH CENTURY, YOU HAVE NEVER TRULY BEEN *ALIVE*.

ALL YOU ARE, DETECTIVE, IS MIRACULOUSLY *NOT DEAD*.

EVEN AMONG MY IMMORTAL BRETHREN...

ARE YOU FAMILIAR, DETECTIVE, WITH THE LEGEND OF THE *HSIEN*? PERHAPS YOU KNOW THE *COLORFUL* WORDS OF LAO TZU AS WRITTEN IN THE *TAO TE CHING*:

"HE WHO HAS GRASPED THE SECRET OF LIFE WILL BE SAFE FROM THE ATTACK OF BUFFALO OR TIGER...AND WHY? BECAUSE HE HAS NO SPOT WHERE DEATH CAN ENTER."

TAOISM HAS ALWAYS BEEN ENAMORED OF THE SUPERNATURAL, AND I BELIEVE IT WAS THE ANCIENT CHINESE WRITER LIEH TZU WHO FIRST GAVE NAME TO WHAT WOULD BECOME A VAST PANTHEON OF SUPPOSED IMMORTALS.

THERE WERE THOUSANDS OF THEM, MANY WHIMSICAL GODLINGS OF BIZARRE AND UNPREDICTABLE POWERS-- ONE, FOR INSTANCE, LED AN ARMY OF MONKEYS, AND MANY WERE ABLE TO PASS THROUGH SOLID ROCK WITHOUT HARM.

BY THE TIME I WAS RESEARCHING THE MATTER IN JAPAN, HOWEVER--WHERE THE IMMORTALS WERE KNOWN AS *SENNIN*--THE BLACK DEATH HAD DEVASTATED EUROPE, AFRICA, AND CHINA, FRIGHTENING HUMANITY INTO A DEDICATION TO SCIENCE THAT INCREASINGLY RIVALED THEIR DEVOTION TO RELIGION.

EVEN PEASANTS LOOKING TO THEIR ANCESTORS FOR GUIDANCE WOULD STOP TO INGEST SPECIFIC MUSHROOMS, PINE RESINS OR CINNABAR, BELIEVING THESE MIGHT STIMULATE ETERNAL YOUTH.

⟨TAKE COMFORT IN THIS, STRANGER--⟩

<--THE WORLD WILL BE BETTER OFF WITHOUT YOU.>

AH, YES, AND PEACHES. THERE WAS A BELIEF THAT IMMORTALITY COULD BE BESTOWED UPON ONE WHO ATE FROM SPECIAL PEACHES.

WE HAVE BEEN VERY SLOW, ON THE OTHER HAND, TO RECOGNIZE OUR IMPACT ON THE ENVIRONMENT AND STILL FAIL TO ACKNOWLEDGE OUR DEPENDENCY.

I, WHO HAVE ALWAYS CRAVED EMPTINESS AND DESOLATION, CHEERED THE COPERNICAN REVOLUTION IN 1543.

ENCHANTED BY THAT NEW, HELIO-CENTRIC VIEW OF OUR UNIVERSE, I FAILED, INITIALLY, TO BE ALARMED BY THE INCREASING POPULARITY OF THE MECHANISTIC PARADIGM.

WHAT DO YOU SUPPOSE IT IS THAT MAKES US SO DETERMINED TO TURN OUR BACK ON THE NATURAL WORLD?

I SUPPOSE YOUR INDISCREET REGARD FOR ALL HUMAN LIFE--NO MATTER HOW USELESS--IS AN ADMIRABLE RESPONSE TO THE ONENESS OF ALL THINGS.

THIS WAY.

MINE'S THE RED PORSCHE IN SPACE THIRTY-EIGHT--

≥COUGH≤

--YOU CAN SAVE IT, CAN'T YOU?

STEVEN!

WHAT?

I PAID A HUNDRED AND TWENTY-FIVE GRAND FOR THAT CAR!

ITS JUST THAT I WOULD ASK YOU TO EXPAND THAT CONCEPT TO ITS NEXT LOGICAL STAGE.

IT IS PERHAPS TRUE THAT NO ONE HUMAN IS DIRECTLY RESPONSIBLE FOR DEFORESTATION, THE GREENHOUSE EFFECT, OR THE SUDDEN HEALTH RECLASSIFICATION OF THE TUNA SANDWICH...

...BUT WE DO EACH HAVE INDIVIDUAL ECOLOGICAL FOOTPRINTS, AND I WOULD THINK IT COUNTERPRODUCTIVE TO RESCUE SOMEONE WHO WAS ACTIVELY DESTROYING YOUR ABODE.

NEXT TIME YOU SAVE A LIFE, DETECTIVE, CONSIDER ASKING A FEW PRUDENT QUESTIONS:

HOW OFTEN DOES YOUR HAPLESS VICTIM EAT MEAT OR PROCESSED FOODS, AND HOW FULL ARE HIS TRASHCANS WHEN HE PUTS THEM OUT ON THE CURB EACH WEEK?

HOW MANY TIMES A WEEK DOES HE INFLICT UPON THE ATMOSPHERE THE FUMES OF HIS INTERNAL COMBUSTION ENGINE? HOW OFTEN DOES HE SQUANDER PRECIOUS FOSSIL FUELS ON SUPERFLUOUS COMFORTS?

‹NO.›

‹NONE OF THIS IS ABOUT ME, SEIOBO. ANY MORE THAN IT IS ABOUT YOU.›

‹*THIS* IS OUR PATIENT.›

‹OUR MOTHER, OUR BODY, OUR *HOME*...›

‹WE KNOW TRICKS-- SMALL CRACKS IN SCIENCE AND NATURE THROUGH WHICH WE HAVE LEARNED TO SLIP-- THAT REJUVENATE OUR BODIES AND MINDS.›

‹BUT NO MORTAL CAN COUNT HIMSELF WORTHY OF INFINITE LIFE WITHOUT A GREATER GOAL SUSTAINING HIS SOUL.›

‹DO YOU KNOW WHAT MAKES ME WORTHY OF INFINITE LIFE, DOCTOR CRUSADER?›

‹THE TRICK OF WHICH YOU SPEAK? THE LITTLE CRACK?›

‹I FOUND IT *FIRST*.›

‹A GREATER GOAL...!?›

‹WHAT GREATER GOAL DO I NEED THAN THE INTENTION NEVER TO *DIE*?›

RA'S AL GHUL
[TRANSLATION: THE DEMON'S HEAD]
REAL NAME: UNKNOWN
HOSTILE
DECEASED: 2004

RA'S WAS A ZEALOUS MEGALOMANIACAL WORLDWIDE ENVIRONMENTAL TERRORIST WHO WAS UNFORTUNATELY ALSO NEARLY IMMORTAL, HAVING AT HIS DISPOSAL THE MYSTERIOUS LAZARUS PITS. IT IS IMPOSSIBLE TO SAY EXACTLY HOW MANY TIMES HE USED THESE MAGICAL WATERS TO REJUVENATE HIS PHYSICAL FORM, BUT IT IS CLEAR THAT HE CARRIES THE WISDOM OF A MAN WHO HAS SEEN MORE THAN A FEW CENTURIES GO BY. OF UNCOMMON STRENGTH AND STAMINA, HE WAS A SKILLED HAND-TO-HAND COMBATANT AND A MASTER SWORDSMAN. HE WAS ALSO NOT ABOVE USING HIS DAUGHTER TALIA AS A WEAPON AND A LURE. RA'S WAS ALSO ONE OF THE FEW ENEMIES TO HAVE DISCOVERED MY SECRET IDENTITY. THE ONLY WAY TO DEFEAT HIM WAS TO REDIRECT HIS FOCUS TO PROTECTION OF THE LAZARUS PITS, ON WHICH HE WAS MORTALLY DEPENDENT.

--DO YOU COPY?

YES, SIR.

IS THE GAS MAIN FIRE STABILIZED?

FOR THE MOMENT.

I NEED YOU TO GO TO MERCY HOSPITAL AND REPORT BACK TO ME ON ADMISSIONS FOR THE PAST FORTY-EIGHT HOURS AND AVAILABLE BED SPACE.

CERTAINLY, SIR.

THOUGH WOULDN'T IT BE QUICKER TO SIMPLY RING THEM?

I NEED AN EYEWITNESS ON THIS, ALFRED.

I THINK RA'S MAY BE TRYING TO GET IN THE LAST WORD FROM BEYOND THE GRAVE...

LESLIE, THANK YOU FOR AGREEING TO MEET ME HERE.

TRUTHFULLY, BRUCE, I WAS HAPPY TO GET AWAY FROM THE CLINIC.

I'VE BEEN SEEING THIS SAME SORT OF THING ALL DAY.

ONCE OR TWICE AND IT'S A HAPPY MIRACLE, A FIGHTER--

--BUT AT SOME POINT, YOU KNOW, DEATH CAN BE A MERCY.

THERE'S NOTHING WE CAN DO FOR SO MANY OF THESE PEOPLE, AND THIS LEVEL OF HOSPITAL CARE WILL QUICKLY BECOME EXPENSIVE AND IMPRACTICAL.

NOT TO MENTION UN-AVAILABLE.

ALFRED'S REPORTING THE SAME KIND OF NUMBERS FROM MERCY.

40

AND MEANWHILE, THE MORGUES ARE EMPTY.

APPARENTLY NO ONE IN GOTHAM HAS DIED FOR GOING ON TWENTY-SIX HOURS NOW.

IN SOME WAYS, IT'S EVERYTHING I'VE EVER WORKED FOR.

BUT NOT LIKE THIS.

NOT CORRUPTED BY RA'S AL GHUL.

RA'S?

BUT I THOUGHT HE WAS FINALLY DEAD...

〈WHY ARE YOU MEN SO IN LOVE WITH DEATH?〉

IMAGINE A SINGLE HUMAN BODY.

SO MANY CELLS, ALL WITH DIFFERENT JOBS TO DO, WORKING IN PERFECT HARMONY TO SUPPORT THE SYSTEM AS A WHOLE.

THIS IS HOW WE DEFINE HEALTH, IS IT NOT?

IF I AM TRULY DEAD, IT IS BECAUSE YOU HAVE DESTROYED THE VERY LAST OF THE LAZARUS PITS IN AN EFFORT TO KEEP ME FROM RISING AGAIN.

AND I'M FLATTERED, REALLY, THAT YOU CONSIDER ME CAPABLE OF FORCING SUCH AN ANOMALY OUT OF THE EARTH...

...JUST AS I AM PLEASED TO BE SO THOROUGHLY ASSOCIATED WITH THEM IN YOUR MIND, AS IF THE SUPPORT OF MY WILL WAS THE ONLY POSSIBLE PURPOSE THEY COULD SERVE.

BY THE TIME YOU ARE READING THIS, HOWEVER, I ASSUME YOU WILL HAVE REALIZED THE EXTENT TO WHICH THAT IS UNTRUE.

THIS IS ADAM-TWELVE WITH AN A.D.D.

IN ADDITION TO OFFICER DOWN, WE'VE GOT MULTIPLES. I REPEAT, MULTIPLES AT THIRD AND KING.

OKAY, JUST--JUST DON'T MOVE.

...JAMIE...

GHAH!

...BATMAN... PLEASE...

...KILL ME....

WHAT THE HELL?

FEAR NO MORE, YOUNG DETECTIVE.

FEAR NO MORE...

BEEP

AARGH!

GO HOME.

ALFRED—

MY DEAR
DETECTIVE—

19 JULY 2001,
CAIRO

THOUGH I CANNOT
HELP BUT HOPE THAT THE
DELIVERY OF THIS LETTER
PROVES UNNECESSARY, I
WRITE IT NOW WITH THE
GREAT COMPASSION AN
RESPECT I HAVE ALWA
FELT TOWARDS YOU.

INTERDEPENDENCY OF ALL
LIFE ON THIS PLANET AND THE
FINAL NECESSITY OF
...ECTING THE LARGER
...NISM OF WHICH WE ARE
...ALL A PART—

...BUT I WOULD BE
...OT TO PLAN FOR
...BILITY
...YOUR
...UR
...Y B...
...A...

IT IS STILL MY
INTENTION TO WIN YOU T
MY CAUSE—NO MAN WI
YOUR INTELLIG
COULD FAIL T
ABSOLUTE

--GOT
ANYTHING?

INDEED, SIR.
YOUR HUNCH WAS
CORRECT.

THERE IS A SECOND
LETTER ENCODED WITHIN
RA'S' FIRST, THIS ONE
IN ARABIC.

I'M WORK-
ING ON THE
TRANSLATION
NOW.

GOOD.

WE'LL NEED
EVERY CLUE WE
CAN GET.

SEND ME
WHAT YOU'VE
GOT.

60

SO INDEED, AS I AM SURE YOU HAVE INFERRED, I DO THINK IT BEST THAT YOU FIND AND OPEN A NEW PIT.

IF FOR SOME REASON YOU CANNOT OPEN ONE ORGANICALLY, I AM CONFIDENT, DETECTIVE, THAT YOU WILL MAKE GOOD USE OF ALL THE WISDOM I PASS ON TO YOU HERE.

AND DO NOT THINK FOR A MOMENT THAT YOU ARE DOING THIS MERELY FOR ME, IN ORDER TO GRANT ME A CHANCE TO RETURN.

I AM PATIENT, AND REALIZE THAT YOU MAY PREFER TO LET THIS ANOMALY PLAY OUT UNTIL ALL OF YOUR DEAD HAVE RISEN.

TAKE YOUR TIME, DETECTIVE. I WILL WAIT UNTIL YOU GROW TIRED....

I WONDER IF YOU REALIZE HOW CLOSE TO IMMORTALITY YOU YOURSELF HAVE STOOD.

I AM NOT REFERRING NOW TO YOUR LEGEND OR THE WORK YOU HAVE DONE, THOUGH BOTH WILL SURELY KEEP YOU IN THE DREAMS AND NIGHTMARES OF MEN FOR CENTURIES TO COME.

NO, DETECTIVE, I AM REFERRING TO THE TANGIBLE ELIXIR OF LIFE YOU NOW SEEK, THE SECRET ALCHEMY OF THE LAZARUS PIT.

YOU HAVE STOOD BY MY SIDE AT THE GATE BEFORE, BUT DID NOT UNDERSTAND WHAT I SOUGHT AT THAT THRESHOLD...

KRAKK

GYAAA!

DETECTIVE.

...TORAY SOHA...

RA'S.

...OM TARA TU TARA...

YOUR "GENOCIDE" SATELLITE WON'T BE LAUNCHING AS PLANNED.

85

SIR?

ALFRED, GO AHEAD.

I AM SO TERRIBLY SORRY TO DISTURB YOU, SIR, BUT YOU ASKED THAT I CONTACT YOU SHOULD THE SITUATION IN THE CITY WORSEN...

...AND INDEED, IT DOES CONTINUE TO DETERIORATE.

ALL THE NEWS STATIONS ARE NOW COVERING THE STORY WITH VARIOUS DEGREES OF ACCURACY, AND IT IS CAUSING MORE THAN A BIT OF PANIC...

"...LOOTING HAS BROKEN OUT EVERYWHERE WITH SPECIAL EMPHASIS ON BASIC RESOURCES SUCH AS FOOD AND WATER..."

"...PEOPLE HAVE BECOME CONVINCED THAT OVERPOPULATION IS IMMINENT, WHICH I SUPPOSE IS ACCURATE.

"TRAVEL IS RAPIDLY BECOMING IMPOSSIBLE, WHAT WITH THE SEEMINGLY ENDLESS INCREASE IN COMMUTERS...

"...AND EVEN SMALL NUISANCES HAVE GROWN IN SUCH PROPORTION AS TO BECOME MAJOR, LEGITIMATE DISTURBANCES."

THERE IS ALSO THE MATTER OF CRIMINALS BECOMING INCREASINGLY EMBOLDENED AND LAW ENFORCEMENT BECOMING INCREASINGLY TAXED...

I UNDERSTAND.

I'VE FINALLY DECODED RA'S' MESSAGES BUT STILL HAVE AT LEAST THREE STOPS TO MAKE BEFORE RETURNING HOME.

IS IT THAT DIFFICULT TO LOCATE A POTENTIAL NEW LAZARUS PIT?

IT'S IMPOSSIBLE.

I FOUND AND DESTROYED THEM ALL BEFORE RA'S' DEATH. NOW I'LL HAVE TO CREATE ONE MYSELF.

AND RA'S HAS LEFT YOU THE MEANS TO DO THIS?

IT WOULD BE IN HIS BEST INTEREST.

AFTER EXAMINING TWO ARTIFACTS RA'S MENTIONED IN HIS LETTERS--THE PEACH OF SEIBO AND THE *MAGNOLIA VIRGINIANA L* PROMINENT ON THE FLORIDA COAST--I CAME UP WITH TWO MAP COORDINATES.

IT'S REASONABLE TO ASSUME THAT I'LL FIND THE MISSING KEY TO THE LAZARUS FORMULA AT THE INDICATED LOCATION...

IT WOULD...

THAT WOULD APPEAR TO ENTAIL BUT ONE STOP...

...OM TARA TU TARA...

...TORAY SOHA...

...GATE GATE PARAGATE...

...PARASAMGATE BODHI SVAHA...

YOU COME AT LAST, INFIDEL!

NOW TELL ME HOW TO CREATE THE PIT SO THAT I CAN BRING BACK MY MASTER, AND YOU CAN RESTORE ORDER TO THIS OVERGROWN WORLD!

...OM TARA TU TARA...

TELL ME!

KRUNNK

CLANG

Gotham Gazette

★★★ ★★★

R.I.P. GOTHAM
CITY'S CORPSES FIND PEACE ONCE AGAIN

by Maureen Michaels

An inexplicable medical crisis came to an end early today with the re-interment of hundreds of recently buried Gotham citizens and a dramatic increase in reported hospital mortality rates. "It really was like death took a holiday," says Dr. William Prince, head of the Gotham General Intensive Care Unit. "Our job here is to save lives whenever possible, but something happened that really threw off the entire balance of existence. I'm sorry for the families who are now losing loved ones after frankly miraculous recoveries, but I'm relieved to see more recognizable fatality patterns reestablishing themselves in the I.C.U."

"We were just over-whelmed," agrees Dr. Femi Opara, medical administrator for the privately-run Saint Mary's medical center in Coventry. "You always want the best for your patients, but we reached a point here where we simply ran out of resources and explanations for what was happening. Even those who were benefiting from it were concerned. What was happening was unnatural." Indeed, speculation concerning possible causes for the sixty-four-hour ban on death and accompanying

temporary reversal of the aging process range from fantastical to conspiratorial, with little in the way of provable hypotheses. "I think Superman must have reversed the planet's spin on its axis," insists Burnley resident Al Evans. "He probably did it to save one particular person, without being aware of the potential side effects."
....continued A6

MICK MORRIGAN, DEAD AGAIN
SURVIVING ELECTRIC CHAIR VICTIM FOUND DEAD IN GROCERY PARKING LOT

By William Baumgarner

Witnesses and officials at Blackgate Prison were stunned last Tuesday when convicted murdered Mick Morrigan not only survived electrocution, but also subsequently broke free of the electric chair and the prison vowing revenge on Gotham City's mysterious Batman, whom Morrigan seemed to blame for his incarceration.

"We've had people survive the initial electrocution once or twice before," admits Blackgate warden Tom Lansky. "But it's usually just a glitch in the machinery that we can fix up pretty fast. With Morrigan, everything was working and we all thought he was dead,
....continued B11

YOU SET THE UBU'S ON A WILD GOOSE CHASE, THAT I UNDERSTAND.

BUT LET ME GET THIS STRAIGHT...

...RA'S' LETTERS LED YOU TO MAP COORDINATES WHERE YOU FOUND A MONK CHANTING THE CHEMICAL FORMULA FOR THE LAZARUS PIT?

HE WAS RECITING A BUDDHIST MANTRA THAT PHONETICALLY CONVERTED INTO A CHEMICAL FORMULA, YES.

I SEE.

AND WITH THAT YOU WERE ABLE TO RECREATE A LAZARUS PIT ANYWHERE, DESPITE HAVING CLOSED OFF ALL THOSE OF NATURAL ORIGIN.

YOU KNOW, I CAN THINK OF SEVERAL SUITABLE LOCATIONS THAT WOULD NOT ENTAIL--

NO.